W9-CFQ-111

CELEBRITY BIOS

Leonardo DiCaprio

by
Kristin McCracken

Children's Press
A Division of Grolier Publishing
New York / London / Hong Kong / Sydney
Danbury, Connecticut

To Susan, my biggest fan

Photo Credits: Cover photo © Sylvia Norris/Globe Photos; pp. 4, 9, 11, 12, 14, 17, 18, 21, 27, 29, 31, 37 © Everett Collection; p. 22 © K.C. Bailey/Everett; p. 24 © Dave Benett/Globe Photos Inc.; p. 38 © Nina Prommer/Globe Photos Inc.

Visit Children's Press on the Internet at:
http://publishing.grolier.com

Library of Congress Cataloging-in-Publication Data

McCracken, Kristin.
  Leonardo DiCaprio / by Kristin McCracken.
    p. cm. – (Celebrity bios)
  Includes bibliographical references and index.
  Summary: A biography of the young California actor who starred in the film "Titanic."
  ISBN 0-516-23323-8 (lib. bdg.) – ISBN 0-516-23523-0 (pbk.)
    1. DiCaprio, Leonardo–Juvenile literature. 2. Motion picture actors and actresses–United States–Juvenile literature. [1. DiCaprio, Leonardo. 2. Actors and actresses.] I. Title. II. Series.

PN2287.D4635 M33 2000
791.43'028'092–dc21
[B]

                                                              99-054074

CONTENTS

CHAPTER ONE

This Boy's Life

"There's always a new pretty face—you definitely want to be remembered for your work rather than being sort of the hunk-of-the-month deal. That's what I've always aimed for." — Leo on "Good Morning America"

As one of Hollywood's biggest stars, Leonardo DiCaprio is admired for both his looks and his talent. How did Leonardo become a superstar? Maybe he was destined to be famous, right down to his famous name . . . .

A STAR IS BORN

Leonardo DiCaprio was named after another famous Leonardo. While on a vacation in Italy, Leonardo's mother, Irmelin, and his father, George, were visiting a museum. Irmelin, who was pregnant, stopped in front of a painting by the Italian artist, Leonardo da Vinci. When baby Leonardo gave a big kick inside her, she decided right then and there to name her son-to-be after the famous painter.

Leonardo Wilhelm DiCaprio was born on November 11, 1974, in Los Angeles, California. His parents divorced when Leo was one year old. He went to live with his mother, but both his parents were involved in raising him. Leo's father is an artist who works with comic books. Leo's mom, who is from Germany, taught Leo how to speak German. He can still speak the language fluently!

YOUNG PERFORMER

Growing up in Hollywood, California, Leo was surrounded by the world of TV and movies.

Leonardo was just two and a half years old when his dad took him to an audition for the kid's TV show, "Romper Room." The show's producers liked Leo's look and energy. Unfortunately, Leonardo was a little too wild for the producers. After just one show, Leo was asked not to come back. That was the one and only time he's been fired from a job!

Leo's stepbrother, Adam, was the person who introduced Leo to acting. Adam had been cast in a TV commercial for Golden Grahams cereal. Thirteen-year-old Leo decided he wanted to try acting professionally, too.

Did you know?

One agent told young Leo to change his name to "Lenny Williams" and get a different haircut. Lucky for us, Leo decided to keep both.

He began asking his mother to take him to auditions for commercials and TV shows.

Leo went to many auditions before he was hired for his first TV commercial. Leo was fourteen years old when he did his first commercial—for Matchbox cars. That same year, he acted in more than twenty commercials and in many educational films.

TEENAGE YEARS

While Leo was acting in commercials, he also was going to school. From seventh to tenth grade, Leo attended the Los Angeles Center for Enriched Studies (LACES). Yet Leo was not well-liked by his teachers or fellow students. His homeroom teacher told *Seventeen,* "[Leo] was a lot more articulate than many of the kids in school and not physically big. He was the odd man out . . . which is tough when you're fifteen."

In 1987, Leo started at John Marshall High School. There he had his first acting role, in a school play called *Circus Fantasy.* Leo continued to

A young Leo

be a difficult student. "He was a brat in my class," his English teacher told *Seventeen*. "He talked back, and I remember sending him to the dean's office fairly often for having attitude problems."

Leo explained his bad behavior in an interview with *Teen*. "I grew up in a pretty tough neighborhood [in Hollywood]. I just had to stay tough myself and develop a plan for doing something better with my life than what the kids were doing around me. I didn't want to waste my life."

Leo discovered that the best way to achieve the life he wanted was through acting. Leo started going on more and more auditions. He finally left John Marshall High School and finished his senior year with a tutor. His mother quit her job as a secretary to help manage Leo's career.

SMALL-SCREEN SUCCESS

In 1989, fifteen-year-old Leo got his first TV role. He had a small part as a troubled boy on "The New Lassie," a Saturday morning kids' show.

"Parenthood" cast from left to right: David Arquette,
Bess Meyer, Maryedith Burrell, Leonardo DiCaprio

Over the next two years, Leo worked on many
other TV shows. In 1990, Leo appeared on the
soap opera "Santa Barbara." He played a teenage
alcoholic. That same year, Leo had small parts on
two TV series, "The Outsiders" and "Parenthood."
He also had a small part on an episode of

Leo with co-star Kirk Cameron on "Growing Pains."

"Roseanne," but the scene was later cut. Leo did get to meet Sarah Gilbert, who played one of Roseanne's daughters. Leo considers Sarah one of his closest friends. In the fall of 1990, Leo also began to appear on the covers of teen magazines.

Leo's regular TV work helped when he auditioned for the 1991 horror movie, *Critters III*. He was just sixteen years old when he got the role. He played a boy who battles furry beasts from outer space. Unfortunately, *Critters III* was not a hit. Even so, a movie is an important credit for an actor to have. Later that year, a hit TV show asked Leo to audition for a small but regular role.

In 1991, Leo joined the cast of the ABC sit-com "Growing Pains." He played Luke Brower, a homeless boy adopted by the show's main char-acters, the Seaver family. "Growing Pains" was canceled in 1992, soon after Leo started. By this time, however, he was ready to leave TV behind him and focus on his film career.

CHAPTER TWO

Rising Star

"He's one of those young men who doesn't want to be a movie star. With Leonardo, it's about the work. He really wants to be known for his acting, not for his looks." —Casting director Mali Finn in *Seventeen*

In 1993, nineteen-year-old Leo auditioned with four hundred other boys for the lead role in the film *This Boy's Life*. Leo was the one who was chosen. He played the writer Tobias Wolff as a teenager. Robert DeNiro was cast as Toby's abusive stepfather. DeNiro is one of Leo's role models, so working with him was a big honor. It was

Leo in *This Boy's Life*

also the first time that Leo played such a large and important film role.

Leo's performance in *This Boy's Life* earned the praise of movie critics across the country. In 1993, the Los Angeles Film Critics Association gave Leo a New Generation Award. That same year, the American Youth Awards presented him with the Actor of the Year award.

Leo liked acting in *This Boy's Life*. He did admit that it was sometimes scary playing an abused child. "It was hard not to get frightened," Leo said on his official Web site. "But I liked it when [DeNiro] scared me. It helped me react." It also prepared Leo for an even more challenging role.

GRAPE EXPECTATIONS

Later that year, Leo auditioned for the movie *What's Eating Gilbert Grape?* starring Johnny Depp and Juliette Lewis. He was cast as a developmentally disabled boy named Arnie.

Roles involving mental disabilities are very

What's Eating Gilbert Grape? starred [from left to right] Leo DiCaprio, Johnny Depp, and Juliette Lewis.

hard for an actor. They are especially difficult for someone as young as Leo. To prepare for the role, Leo spent time with children who had

Leo as the developmentally disabled Arnie

developmental disabilities. He was able to get a
better idea of what these children were like. He
also watched videos of young people who were

similar to Arnie. This preparation was very help-ful for Leo. "People have these expectations that mentally [challenged] children are really crazy and out there," Leo explained on his official Web site. "But it's refreshing to see them because everything's always so new to them. Playing Arnie was so much fun because everything I did was so unexpected."

What's Eating Gilbert Grape? was not a box-office hit. Still, people in the film industry liked young Leo's performance. In 1993, the National Board of Review, an important film group, gave Leo the Best Supporting Actor Award. The Los Angeles Film Critics Association gave Leo a sec-ond New Generation Award. Leo was also nomi-nated for a Golden Globe that year. But his most important nomination was yet to come.

WHAT AN HONOR!

In 1994, the Academy of Motion Picture Arts and Sciences decided to honor Leo. They nominated him for an Academy Award, or Oscar, for his performance as Arnie. An Oscar is one of the greatest honors a film actor can receive for a performance. Some actors work for decades and never get an Oscar nomination. Leo was selected at the age of nineteen.

Leo was very nervous on the night of the Academy Awards. He explained to *Teen*, "I was so nervous [Oscar] night. I almost would rather not have been nominated! I was almost sick. Especially when people kept telling me I might surprise everyone and win."

Leo didn't win the Oscar that year. Still, once an actor has been nominated, he or she becomes very popular in Hollywood. Leonardo was no exception. Soon people all over the world were sending him movie scripts. They hoped Leo would agree to be in their next project. The boy who once begged his mother to let him work in commercials now had his pick of movie roles.

Leo in "The Quick and the Dead"

A BUSY YEAR

Leo acted in three films in 1995. Each film gave him the chance to play a very different character. In *The Quick and the Dead*, Leonardo starred as a hotshot cowboy called The Kid. He acted opposite Sharon Stone, who played a mysterious gunfighter. Audiences did not rush to the theaters to

Leo in *The Basketball Diaries*

see this western, however. *The Quick and the Dead* died at the box office very quickly.

Leo's next film was *The Basketball Diaries*. It was about troubled youths in New York City. Leo played Jim Carroll, a young poet and basketball player who became a drug addict. The movie was not a box office hit, but critics praised Leo's performance. Leo and his co-star, Mark Wahlberg, also got to be good friends. In *Jump*, Wahlberg described Leo as "the most down-to-earth person I've ever met—very un-Hollywood."

Leo's preference for playing odd characters led to his third film in 1995. He starred in the very un-Hollywood *Total Eclipse*. The movie was filmed in France with a mostly unknown cast. Leonardo played the famous nineteenth-century French poet, Arthur Rimbaud. Rimbaud may have been popular in France, but the movie didn't do well in the United States. *Total Eclipse* was another box-office flop.

Leo was worried. It looked as though his movie career was on the rocks. But just one year later, everything would change.

CHAPTER THREE

A Leading Man

"It's a weird feeling when people are defining you, and you haven't even defined yourself . . . I don't even know who I am yet, or what kind of actor I want to be. I'm still in a stage of discovery." —Leo on *E!Online*

In 1996, Leo signed on to play Romeo, the most famous teenage heartthrob of all time. The movie was *Romeo + Juliet*. It was based on William Shakespeare's most well-known play. This new version starred Leo and Claire Danes as the pair of doomed young lovers.

Set in present-day Florida, *Romeo + Juliet* was

Leo with his *Romeo + Juliet* co-star, Claire Danes

exciting, colorful, and loud. The movie looked almost like a music video. It was full of action, and the story raced along toward its tragic end. The young stars gave the film the biggest boost of all. Teen audiences knew Claire Danes from the TV show "My So-Called Life." Leo's face had been in teen magazines for several years. Romeo was Leo's first romantic "leading man" role. Audiences had decided that Leo was indeed the perfect new Romeo.

In its opening weekend, *Romeo + Juliet* became the number-one movie in America. For the first time, Leo was a movie star who was actually in a hit movie. Suddenly, women everywhere recognized this handsome young man. Audiences were excited to see what Leo would do next.

ANOTHER HIT

Before the release of *Romeo + Juliet*, Leo finished the film *Marvin's Room*. Leo once again got to work with Robert DeNiro. Leo also got the

Leo starred with Meryl Streep in *Marvin's Room*.

chance to perform with two Academy Award-winning actresses, Diane Keaton and Meryl Streep. In the film, Leo played Hank, a (what else?) troubled teenager. Hank had a strange love of fire. Although not as popular as *Romeo + Juliet*, 1996's *Marvin's Room* was still a solid hit. The Screen Actors Guild, which is made up of the world's most famous actors, honored Leo. The Guild gave him an Outstanding Performance nomination for his role in *Marvin's Room*.

SAILING TO STARDOM

Even before filming began in early 1996, it was clear that the movie *Titanic* was going to be either a huge hit or a complete flop. The film's producers knew they had to find the perfect actor for the lead role of Jack Dawson. With his recent success as Romeo, Leo was an obvious choice. The film's director, James Cameron, wasn't so sure. "I actually didn't want Leo at first," recalled Cameron on Leo's official Web site. "He was recommended by the studios, as were other young, hot actors, but he just didn't strike me as having the qualities I wanted for my

Did you know?

Leo tried out to play Robin, the Boy Wonder, in the 1997 movie, *Batman and Robin.* He lost the role to Chris O'Donnell. Leo later beat out O'Donnell for the lead role in *Titanic.*

Leonardo with *Titanic* director James Cameron and co-star Kate Winslet at the Golden Globe Awards.

Jack." Once the director saw Leo's audition, though, he immediately changed his mind. Cameron said of Leo, "I loved him! He can quickly charm a group of people without doing anything obvious. The second I met him, I was completely convinced." Cameron found his Jack Dawson, and the rest is history.

Titanic became the most successful movie of all time. For his performance, Leo received a Golden Globe nomination for Best Actor. He also won best actor awards at the MTV Movie Awards and the Blockbuster Awards. Leo was not nominated for an Academy Award, but *Titanic* did win eleven Oscars, including Best Picture of 1997. Audiences all over the world were thrilled by the special effects of the sinking ship. Most of all, they fell in love with the romantic and tragic story of Rose and Jack.

LIFE AFTER *TITANIC*

Titanic was the number-one movie in the United States for almost five months. The only movie that could knock *Titanic* from the top spot was Leo's next film, *The Man in the Iron Mask*. In this 1998 movie, Leonardo played two roles. He portrayed the evil King Louis XIV of France. He also played the king's twin brother, Philippe, who is locked away in prison for six years.

The Man in the Iron Mask was Leo's tenth film in just four years. After he finished the movie, Leo promised himself that he would take a vaca-

Leo played two roles in *The Man in the Iron Mask*. He is pictured here as Philippe, the jailed brother of the king.

tion. Then he got an offer he couldn't turn down. He was given the chance to work with the famous director Woody Allen. Leo was a big fan of Woody Allen's movies. Leo agreed to play a small role, also called a cameo, in the director's 1998 movie, *Celebrity*. Leo only had fifteen minutes of screen time. Still, Leo thought it was a fun character to play. His role was that of a famous movie star who throws temper tantrums and treats people badly. Leo assured people that he was only acting. He is nothing like that character at all!

WATER WATER EVERYWHERE

Leo considered many projects for 1999. He finally decided to do a film called *The Beach*. "I waited quite a while for my next movie because I wanted to truly find a project I was in love with," Leo told *Cinema* magazine.

In January 1999, Leo traveled to Thailand, a country in Asia, to start filming *The Beach*. He played the part of Richard, a traveler who winds up living on a remote desert island. The adventure movie also had plenty of romantic scenes between Leo and his French co-star, Virginie Ledoyen.

CHAPTER FOUR

Fame, Fortune, and the Real Leo

"The last thing I want to do is turn into a Hollywood jerk. I don't think I'll strive for money or success and end up greedy or big-headed. That only leads to unhappiness."
—Leo in *Teen*

At age twenty-five, Leonardo DiCaprio is one of the world's biggest superstars. He's also one of the most complicated. Leo is shy in many ways. He avoids doing interviews and photo shoots. Yet Leo is often spotted out in public. He shows up at the trendiest nightclubs with different super-models on his arm. Those close to Leo know him as a down-to-earth person who loves his friends and family. So just who is the real Leo?

LEO-MANIA

Hotel break-ins, mobs of screaming girls, police officers in riot gear—sound like the latest action movie? Nope, it's just Leo at a movie premiere in Tokyo, Japan. Or it's Leo at an art museum in France. "If my fans really knew me, they wouldn't be impressed," Leo explained to the *Calgary Sun*. "They're reacting to my screen persona (image), not the real me."

Leo insists that deep down, he is just a regular person. Yet it's impossible for Leo even to walk down the street without people wanting to talk to him, take his picture, or get an autograph. This loss of privacy is sometimes difficult for him.

Did you know?

One of Leo's worst habits is biting his nails.

"My mistake is that I think I can actually be like a normal human being and have fun and go to normal places," Leo told the *New York Post*. "I'm realizing that I have to lead a sheltered life where I watch out for everything I do."

KEEPING IT REAL

So how does someone who's surrounded by money, fame, and supermodels manage to stay normal? "The main thing for me is to live life with my family and friends," Leo explained to *Teen*. "That's all I need to keep my sanity."

Leo remains very close to his parents. In fact, until he was twenty-two years old, Leonardo lived with his mother in Los Feliz, California. Los Feliz is the Los Angeles neighborhood where Leo grew up. He finally bought his own house nearby, in Santa Monica, California. Leo also keeps the friendships he had before he was famous. His long-time friends include actors Jay Ferguson and Tobey Maguire, star of the movie *Ride with the Devil.*

When he's away filming a movie, Leo regularly writes letters to his friends. Occasionally he even flies them out to movie sets to visit him. "Leo loves his friends, and he's so loyal to them. And they return the favor," said his *Titanic* co-star, Kate Winslet, in *Teen*. "If Leo needed me any-where tomorrow, I'd be there. Once you're friends with Leo, it's like he's a part of you."

GIVING BACK

Leo is not only generous with his friends and family. He also works with many charities, such as the Make-A-Wish Foundation. The foundation grants the wishes of youths with life-threatening illnesses. He also helps with relief efforts for the homeless. He supports AIDS charities and speaks out for environmental protection.

Leo has not forgotten his hometown, either. The DiCaprio family paid for the construction of a high-tech computer and multimedia center at the Los Feliz Public Library. The Leonardo

Leo may be a superstar, but he is also very loyal to his friends.

DiCaprio Computer Center opened in June 1999. The center is located on the site where Leo's childhood home once stood.

Leo signing autographs for his fans.

WHAT'S IN THE FUTURE?

Leo plans to star in another movie with Robert DeNiro. The film is about Irish and Italian street gangs in New York City during the 1800s.

There are many rumors about what other films Leo will be involved in. His production company bought the movie rights to the book *Dreamland*. Leo is considering playing the lead character, Kid Twist.

Is Leo planning another picture on the same huge scale of *Titanic*? It's not likely, he told *Teen*. "I figure that [doing] something like [*Titanic*] again isn't for me. I may go back on that decision sometime, but for now I want to do things that really appeal to me." What is certain is that Leo will continue to choose interesting and surprising roles. From teenage runaway to Romeo to *Titanic's* leading man, Leonardo DiCaprio is sure to remain one of Hollywood's brightest stars.

TIMELINE

1974   •   Leonardo Wilhelm DiCaprio is born in Los Angeles.

1977   •   Leo auditions for "Romper Room."

1988   •   Leo is cast in his first commercial (Matchbox cars).

1989   •   Leo lands his first TV role on "The New Lassie."

1990   •   Leo appears on the soap opera "Santa Barbara" and the TV shows "Parenthood" and "The Outsiders."

1991   •   Leo lands a regular role on the TV sitcom "Growing Pains."
        •   Leo has his first movie role in *Critters III*.

1993   •   Leo stars in *This Boy's Life* with Robert DeNiro.
        •   Leo plays Arnie Grape in *What's Eating Gilbert Grape?*
        •   Leo wins two New Generation Awards from the Los Angeles Film Critics Association for *What's Eating Gilbert Grape?* and *This Boy's Life*.
        •   Leo receives a Best Supporting Actor Award from the National Board of Review. He is nominated for a Golden Globe for *What's Eating Gilbert Grape?*

1994   •   Leo is nominated for an Academy Award for his performance in *What's Eating Gilbert Grape?*
        •   Leo acts in a short film called *The Foot Shooting Party*.
        •   Leo wins the American Youth Awards Actor of the Year award for *This Boy's Life*.

1995	• Leo stars in *The Quick and the Dead, The Basketball Diaries,* and *Total Eclipse.*
	• Leo appears briefly in the French film *Les Cent et une Nuits.*
1996	• Leo is cast as Romeo in *Romeo + Juliet.*
	• Leo stars in *Marvin's Room.*
	• Leo wins Favorite Romance Actor at the Blockbuster Awards for *Romeo + Juliet.*
1997	• Leo stars as Jack Dawson in *Titanic.*
1998	• Leo plays twins in *The Man in the Iron Mask.*
	• Leo has a cameo role in Woody Allen's *Celebrity.*
	• For his role as Jack Dawson, Leo wins Best Male Actor at the MTV Movie Awards, the American MovieGoer Award for Best Actor, and Favorite Actor at the Blockbuster Awards. He also receives a Golden Globe nomination for Best Actor.
1999	• Leo films *The Beach* in Thailand.
	• Leo signs on to play opposite Robert DeNiro in a movie about nineteenth-century street gangs.

FACT SHEET

Name	Leonardo Wilhelm DiCaprio
Born	November 11, 1974
Birthplace	Los Angeles, California
Family	Parents divorced; Mother: Irmeline, Father: George, Grandmother: Helena, Stepbrother: Adam
Sign	Scorpio
Hair	Blond
Eyes	Blue-green
Height	6 feet
Weight	140 pounds
Shoe Size	11
Pet	Dragon lizard named Blizz
Car	Black Chevy Tahoe

Favorites

Actors	Robert DeNiro, Jack Nicholson, Al Pacino
Actress	Meg Ryan
Book	*The Old Man and the Sea* by Ernest Hemingway
Movies	All three Godfather films
TV Show	"The Twilight Zone"
Food	Pasta
Drinks	Lemonade, Diet Coke, and Fruitopia
Music	Led Zeppelin, The Beatles, Pink Floyd, and rap
Teams	L.A. Lakers (basketball), N.Y. Mets (baseball)
Hobbies	Lifting weights, seeing and buying art

NEW WORDS

agent a person who uses his or her contacts in the entertainment field to get a performer invited to auditions

audition a try-out performance in hopes of getting a role in a movie or TV show

cameo a part in a movie or TV show that is very small

commercial an advertisement for a product that airs on television or radio

critic someone who gives his or her opinion of a movie, TV show, or play

developmental disability a condition that prevents someone from developing normally

director the person in charge of creating a movie, play, or TV show

leading man main male character in a film

multimedia center an area that offers many types of media, including newspapers, computers, and television

nomination selection of someone for an award

Oscar also called an Academy Award; given for outstanding achievement in film

persona image

producer the person who supervises and finances the production of a film or television program

role a character or part played by a performer in a movie or TV show

sitcom television comedy, usually thirty minutes in length

soap opera a television drama that airs in continuous episodes

western a movie, TV show, or book that deals with life in the western United States

FOR FURTHER READING

Bego, Mark. *Leonardo DiCaprio: Romantic Hero.*
Kansas City, MO: Andrews McMell Publishing,
1998.

Krulik, Nancy E. *Leonardo DiCaprio: A Biography.*
New York: Archway, 1998.

Looseleaf, Victoria. *Leonardo: Up Close and
Personal.* New York: Ballantine Books, 1998.

Thompson, Douglas. *Leonardo DiCaprio.* New York:
The Berkley Publishing Group, 1998.

RESOURCES

Web Sites

The Official Leonardo DiCaprio Web Site
www.leonardodicaprio.com
Includes photos, news updates, and links to other Leo
Web sites. Has scenes from upcoming films, a chat
room, and information about joining Leo's fan club.

Romeo + Juliet
www.romeoandjuliet.com
Includes information about the making of the movie,
details about the cast, and a chat room.

Titanic
www.titanicmovie.com
Includes photos and interviews with the film's stars.
Has details about the making of the film. Includes
links to information about the real Titantic disaster.

You can also write to Leo at the following address:

Leonardo DiCaprio
P.O. Box 27008
Los Angeles, CA 90027

INDEX

ABOUT THE AUTHOR

Kristin McCracken is an educator and writer living in New York City. Her favorite activities include seeing movies, plays, and the occasional star on the street.